CW00820920

Enlightenment - Mother to Daughter

Shehnaaz Asaria

Published by Clink Street Publishing 2021

Copyright © 2021

First edition.

The author asserts the moral right under the Copyright, Designs and Patents Act 1988 to be identified as the author of this work.

ISBN:
978-1-912850-74-7 - paperback
978-1-912850-75-4 - ebook

Dearest Kush

With all best Wishes

love Shehnaaz xx

Contents

Forward

I would like to thank my family for their patience whilst I have managed to "free" myself from emigrational, cultural, religious, and social practices by which, many people wished me to abide by.

The journey which I embarked upon in "freeing" myself has resulted in the development of my "personal classification of an individual's personality which I have named "Personal Personality Types (PPTs)".

Shehnaaz Asaria

BOOK 1

The Child

Chapter 1

In this First Book of this Compendium of 3 Books, collectively entitled "Enlightenment - Mother to Daughter", I will talk primarily about the unborn child. It is with much regret that I write that in my humble opinion; the outcome of any child, if it is not taken seriously enough when the child is thought of, and thereafter conceived, can have disastrous consequences.

It is my fervent hope that the following chapters are read with great care, and if necessary read again, to understand the messages in them in their entirety.

I will endeavour to highlight the various junctures in the lives of the parents to be, where in my humble opinion; they can reflect and take steps to ensure that the child they are about to conceive will have the greatest chance of fulfilling its life to its highest potential.

It is with this aim in mind that I start this book with thinking of the parents to be, and how in my humble opinion; they can ensure this by firstly thinking about themselves, that is, by purifying themselves in every meaning of the word, such that their beings are in unison with each other, their thought processes cohesive, and their bodily functions at the highest level to create a child, both in body and mind, having the greatest chance of survival in the world at large, not just when born, but also further on in life, at any stage in its life, from birth to its final demise.

I will also talk about parenthood and how in my humble opinion; the type and quality of parenting from preconception to giving birth, to subsequent years, can affect the child's well-being and ability to cope with life, as well as its mental and physical states. It is in my humble opinion; of paramount importance to understand that, it is not only after giving birth that parenting begins, as it is the states of mind and physical body of the parents to be prior to conceiving, which will, in my humble opinion; also determine the emotional and physical state of the subsequent newborn.

In my humble opinion; one has to understand that at conception, the emotional and physical states of the parents to be have an immense impact, as if these are compromised at all, in my humble opinion; the child will be born with defects of sort, as well as hereditary defects that may inherently going to be present.

It is therefore in my humble opinion; the responsibility of anyone wishing to have a baby to give their intended child the best possible start in life. In my humble opinion; the emotional and physical states of the parents to be are under the jurisdiction of the parents to be, and in my humble opinion; these have to be given enough thought prior to conceiving, as in my humble opinion; parents at odds not only with each other, and/or in my humble opinion; with other family members, colleagues, friends, home helps, and other acquaintances leading to unresolved discords in interpersonal relationships can but in my humble opinion; lead only to their compromised emotional and physical states.

It is with this understanding in my humble opinion; that both parents to be should in my humble opinion; primarily together and of course individually too, in my humble opinion; evaluate their emotional and physical states, and in my humble opinion; to question whether anything in any relationship, be it in my humble opinion; with each other or with other family members, colleagues, friends, home helps, and other acquaintances needs improving, and if changes need to be made, then to take steps to do so as any dilemmas in any relationship in my humble opinion; can but only compromise the ideal emotional and physical states of the parents to be and in my humble opinion; subsequently those of the child to be born as well.

If any aspect or aspects of any relationship under scrutiny, be it between the parents and/or with other family members, colleagues, friends, home helps, and other acquaintances cannot be resolved, then to consider the outcome or outcomes, but also to agree with the relevant party or parties in question not to revisit the discord or discords again as bringing past resentment or resentments to the surface again in my humble opinion; can but only disturb the mental and physical states of the parents to be and in my humble opinion; subsequently those of the child to be born as well.

Once both physical and emotional states of the parents to be have been considered, then the parents to be have to evaluate the well-being of other family members, colleagues, friends, and any other acquaintances as their emotional and physical states will impact the child as it grows in their midst.

No one child is only the parents. The upbringing and growth of a child is a cumulative result of all the combined efforts of the parents, other family members, friends, colleagues, home helps, and any other acquaintances. It is important to understand that the interpersonal relationships of all these people not only with each other but also with the parents to be will play a great part in the happy development of the child.

Parents need to not only question each other of their relationship but their relationships with any family members, friends, colleagues, home helps, and any other acquaintances, especially those that are going to be more in contact with their intended child and ideally before conception make an effort to question and rectify each one if necessary, such that all major relationships are harmonious and conflict free as possible, as any conflict in my humble opinion; can be embedded in some way in the DNA of the child.

So after the parents have made sure that their relationships with family members, friends, colleagues, home helps, and any other acquaintances are at their best, then they can start thinking about their own physical state and their own health.

Any individual's overall health depends on the balance of one's total being which consists in my humble opinion; of five components, with the ultimate balance of, leading to ultimate health. These five components, namely, physical, emotional, mental, spiritual, and social when in balance can lead to a state of personal happiness too.

It is therefore in my humble opinion; of paramount importance that the parents to be not only consider all five aspects of their beings, namely physical, emotional, mental, spiritual and social before conceiving but also the physical, emotional, mental, spiritual and social states of family members, friends, colleagues, home helps, and any other acquaintances as it is in my humble opinion; the combined overall health of all individuals around the parents to be that will affect the overall health of the parents to be, and subsequently the overall health of the child to be born. It is in my humble opinion; that there should be maintenance of balance within the physical, emotional, mental, spiritually and social states of all individuals around the growing child to ensure the child's overall health and into adulthood.

I cannot stress enough, in my humble opinion; the importance of all preparations as detailed in this chapter by the parents to be such that the child is born in an environment where it can flourish and thrive, as well as feel supported into adulthood, and as a result of which will in my humble opinion; be able to replicate in turn.

It is at this point in this chapter, that I would like to highlight that in my humble opinion; that the child to be born is that of the parents, and should therefore be brought up according to the wishes of the couple, and it is only the advice and support of family members, friends, colleagues, home helps, and any other acquaintances that is necessary when sought for, and under no circumstance must the views and opinions of family members, friends, colleagues, home helps, and, any other acquaintances take precedence to, those, of, the parents, and should this not be the status quo, then in my humble opinion; conflict can only but arise hindering the child's progress.

Once it is established that the parents are indeed taking all the decisions for the child until it reaches maturity to take its own decisions, then family members, friends, colleagues, home helps, and any other acquaintances can play their pivotal roles in the child's life under the jurisdiction of the parents.

It is of the utmost importance in my humble opinion; for the parents to be to consider all the points raised in this chapter and should they not be able to find that they are in agreement in the way they are going to raise their child, or if they are unable to make family members, friends, colleagues, home helps, and any other acquaintances understand the need for their direction in the upbringing of their child, then they must in my humble opinion; take steps in leaving the prevailing circumstances such that the child is not affected.

Chapter 2

Following on from our earlier discussions in Chapter 1 of Book 1, in this Compendium of 3 Books, collectively entitled "Enlightenment - Mother to Daughter", about the parents to be being in appropriate health and environment prior to conceiving, it is also in my humble opinion; also of equal importance for this environment to become a permanent feature in their lives, as it is this constancy that will enable for the happy and healthy development of the newborn.

The child is also so very time consuming with constant demands for its care and nurturing, that in my humble opinion; not only have all the pointers raised in Chapter 1 of this Compendium of 3 Books, collectively entitled "Enlightenment - Mother to Daughter" got to be in place, but actually almost as second nature, such that once the child is born, the parents' efforts can be concentrated on the child, and not the setting up of best practice for themselves, the child, family members, colleagues, friends, home helps, and other acquaintances those, around, themselves, having said this, it is in my humble opinion; vital as with all best practices, to constantly check in on them, and make sure they are at their best.

Every time a child is born, best practices in my humble opinion; to maintain health together with ideologies in child rearing will have been developed, that it is vital in my humble opinion; for the parents to be to research into them as well as scrutinise them till they are convinced of their validity. It is also in my humble opinion; as important for them to reflect on the age-old practices of other family members, colleagues, friends, home helps, and any other acquaintances around them and note of any merits in them, and in turn to make an informed plan on how they will undertake the responsibility of the upbringing of their child.

Chapter 3

As discussed in Chapters 1 and 2, of Book 1, in this Compendium of 3 Books, collectively entitled "Enlightenment - Mother to Daughter" that it is of the utmost importance to consider the parents viewpoints at all times, having said, it is in my humble opinion; incumbent for the parents to consider the role of the grandparents as second to none during the lifetime of the child.

It is also my humble opinion; important to incorporate as many other family members, friends, colleagues, home helps, and any other acquaintances into the child's close environment, such that the child can draw valuable experience and ideologies from them.

Chapter 4

In the upbringing of a child, the parents to be, as discussed in Chapter 1, of Book 1, in this Compendium of 3 Books, collectively entitled "Enlightenment - Mother to Daughter" have in my humble opinion; a responsibility to research best practices in all areas of childcare.

Once the child in my humble opinion; is aged 3, it can be taught how to behave and to engage in formal education. It is my humble opinion; that from that age, also to treat the child as an adult and take its views and opinions into consideration when making decisions concerning the family.

It is of utmost importance in my humble opinion; that the child is considered as a unique individual and that the parents recognise the child's strengths and to nurture them accordingly.

In my humble opinion; the way to understand the child's strengths, is to expose the child to a myriad of different activities, and note where the child shows the most interest, having said, in my humble opinion, this should not only be within the parents trajectories, but also in the trajectories of other family members, colleagues, friends, home helps, and any other acquaintances.

Chapter 5

This chapter deals with various aspects of child rearing. In my humble opinion; the child at any age, has the right to express its viewpoints and desires for its own life together with the expectation that its parents, other family members, colleagues, friends, home helps, and other acquaintances will ensure suitable support systems.

It is often the case that within any household, there may be more than one viewpoint, and for relationships to be harmonious, it is important that all members of the household respect each others' boundaries and visions for their own lives and futures.

Chapter 6

In my humble opinion, a child, aged six plus must engage with family members, colleagues, friends, home helps, and other acquaintances knowing the difference between right and wrong.

Chapter 7

By the age of twelve, the child should in my humble opinion; be able to discern what course it wants to follow in its own life.

To conclude, if all the points discussed in this first book are practised by the child, its parents, other family members, colleagues, friends, home helps, and other acquaintances, then in my humble opinion; the child will attain maturity by aged twelve and play a pivotal role in any society.

BOOK 2

Values

Chapter 1

In Book 1, I mainly wrote about the "Child". In this book, that is Book 2 of this Compendium of 3 Books, collectively entitled "Enlightenment - Mother to Daughter", I will engage in highlighting, in my humble opinion; practices to encourage both parents to feel empowered in their own personalities.

A matter to ponder over at this stage in my humble opinion; is that although a child may be born in a certain environment, that is with its parents, other family members, colleagues, friends, home helps, and other acquaintances, its environment as a consequence of globalisation can alter, and as a result it is imperative in my humble opinion to exercise noteworthy discretionary measures outlined in all the chapters of Book 1.

It is from my experience that I write that in the majority of western cultures the role of child care is somewhat equal divided between both parents nowadays, as well as shared with other family members, colleagues, friends, home helps, and other acquaintances. Again, from my experience of eastern cultures, the role of rearing the child is borne mainly by the mother. It is my aim in writing this book, that is Book 2 of this Compendium of 3 Books, collectively entitled "Enlightenment - Mother to Daughter", to in my humble opinion; help both western and eastern cultures to understand the differences in role gender, and for both parents to be able to navigate any unfair practices adopted by their forefathers, and adopt practices that in my humble opinion; are such that neither parent feels sidelined, and can continue with their life choices.

Chapter 2

In this chapter, I would like to in my humble opinion; to impart the necessity for the immediate family unit, that is, the parents and the children to act as a cohesive unit by supporting each other in their individual endeavours, in which each member knows the priorities of the other members. It is in my humble opinion; that in doing so, the children will feel that this immediate family unit will be the closest point of contact during their lifetime.

In my experience of eastern cultures, I have noted that children have to fend financially for themselves from a much earlier age, as they cannot rely on the state or the parents, as more often than not, the state does not have a welfare system in place, and the parents also, more often than not, do not have adequate financial means, this in my experience leading to the majority of children in eastern cultures entering the workplace earlier than their western counterparts.

Consequentially, the children of eastern cultures are in my experience somewhat more understanding of other family members needs from a much earlier age.

Chapter 3

The aim of this chapter is to impart in my humble opinion; values to aspire for; namely freedom, safety, health and happiness. I talk about these values in this chapter, that is, Chapter 3 of Book 2, in this Compendium of 3 books collectively entitled "Enlightenment - Mother to Daughter", as a means to enlighten the reader, in my humble opinion; of their need.

It is in my humble opinion; that these values are obtainable by following the ideologies presented as a collection in all 4 books of this Compendium.

Chapter 4

In any individual's life there are many decisions to be made. The following chapters in this book, that is Book 2, in this Compendium of 3 books collectively entitled "Enlightenment - Mother to Daughter" will in my humble opinion; concentrate on the major instances to consider for consistency in a free, safe, healthy and happy life.

The first of these which will be discussed is that of child birth. It is in my humble opinion; that the mother of the child to be born should make the decision as to which grandmother of the child to have in close proximity as her support system, as well as other family members, colleagues, friends, home helps, and other acquaintances.

It must be borne in mind that in my humble opinion; both parents must be the main support systems to each other at this special time, having said in my humble opinion; it is important in the new parents' lives to have not only the company of, but also the presence of other people that both parents can rely on.

In my humble opinion; the infant's father must at this point empathise and understand the immense strain a pregnancy can have on the mother, both emotionally and physically.

It is also in my humble opinion; that both parents do not forget the commitment they made to each other as partners prior to the birth of the child, and maintain their interest in other.

Prior to deciding to conceive a child, it is imperative in my humble opinion; that the parents to be discuss childcare responsibilities such that post childbirth provisions are in place to ensure both parents feel empowered to not only be parents but also individual's in their own right.

Chapter 5

In my humble opinion; this chapter will discuss another important topic that any relationship needs to clarify prior to solidifying, that being of joint finances.

In my humble opinion; both parents need to disclose all personal wealth to each other, and have discussions for not only their household expenses, but also for the child, themselves, as well as for other family members, colleagues, friends, home helps, and other acquaintances, together with financial discussions for any commitments they may make to their children in their adulthood, as well as their own retirement.

It is in my experience; that finances can have a degree of fluctuation, having said it is in my humble opinion; important for both parents to discuss finances on a monthly basis to maintain family harmony.

Chapter 6

This chapter will deal with the importance of social connections. In my humble opinion; I feel a lineage of the relationships starting with the most important should be always looked at and reflected on, again on a monthly basis, such that one's worth together with one's "giving" is kept in check.

In my humble opinion; the most important relationship after one's Lord is that with oneself;

Then with one's partner;

Then with one's children;

Then with one's parents;

Then with one's siblings;

Then with one's extended family;

Then with one's colleagues;

Then with one's friends;

Then with one's home helps;

Then with one's other acquaintances.

Chapter 7

This chapter deals with the topic of "narcissism" and the degree of presence in an individual, which in my experience and humble opinion; is the result of an individual's upbringing, aged 12 till.

It is in my experience and in my humble opinion; a necessity to examine the degree of "narcissism" present in individuals; whether it be a life partner, other family members, colleagues, friends, home helps, and other acquaintances, such that one's self worth is not compromised.

It is in my experience and humble opinion; that individuals display varying degrees of "narcissism", the traits of which in my experience and humble opinion can include up to eight of the following:

1. The need to feel more important than the other
2. The need to feel more valued than the other
3. The need to have more interest in themselves than the other
4. The need to have greater self worth than the other
5. The need to have more time spent on themselves than the other
6. The need to have self pity
7. The need to never show any interest in the other
8. The need to always talk about themselves

It is in my experience and humble opinion; that individual's displaying any number of the above characteristics cannot actually rectify their behavioural patterns, and it is also from

my experience and humble opinion; that consequential actions
to question any of the above 8 traits can only but lead to further
exacerbation in relationship disharmonies to include;

1. Further belittling of the questioner
2. Further demeaning of the questioner
3. Further controlling measures of the questioner
4. Further exclusion of the questioner
5. Further demoralisation of the questioner
6. Further subjugation of the questioner
7. Further restrictive measures towards the questioner
8. Further public humiliation of the questioner

BOOK 3

Relationships

Chapter 1

In this Third Book of this Compendium of 3 Books, collectively entitled "Enlightenment - Mother to Daughter", I will explain a new way of understanding peoples' personalities, developed by myself, called "Personal Personality Types (PPTs)".

In my humble opinion; all individuals can be categorised by one of the following 9 PPTs; 1. SoftSoftSoft 2. SoftSoft 3. Soft 4. MediumSoft 5. Medium 6. MediumHard 7. MediumHardEgoist 8. Hard 9. HardHard.

In my humble opinion; it is of paramount importance to discover any individual's authentic PPT, to be able to manage any relationship, be it with family members, colleagues, friends, home helps, and other acquaintances.

It is from my experience and in my humble opinion; that an individual's PPT is the consequence of the amount of "ABSOLUTE LOVE" shown to that individual in its formative first twelve years by family members, colleagues, friends, home helps, and other acquaintances.

It is at this juncture that I would like to impart in my experience and humble opinion; my definition of "ABSOLUTE LOVE" as being an existence where an individual in its formative first twelve years is shown all *"5 Languages of Love by Gary Chapman"* by family members, colleagues, friends, home helps, and other acquaintances. Gary Chapman describes these as words of affirmation, quality time, receiving gifts, acts of service and physical touch.

It is from my experience and in my humble opinion; that individuals are shown various degrees of ABSOLUTE LOVE" during their formative first twelve years and as a result they fall into one of the 9 PPTs.

It is from my experience and in my humble opinion; that an individual who has a Soft PPT is one that has experienced "ABSOLUTE LOVE" in its formative first twelve years from its family members, colleagues, friends, home helps, and other acquaintances, having said, that child also has not been overindulged.

It is from my experience and in my humble opinion; that the Soft Individual is one that has a balance between providing for themselves and others, such that they can view the world compassionately, and in terms of "giving to others"; is generous with time, empathetic in language to encourage, fosters relationships with helpful suggestions, and for themselves; enables enough encounters to enrich their life and is able to focus such that they can have continual growth.

It is from my experience and in my humble opinion; that an individual with a SoftSoftSoft PPT has experienced "ABSOLUTE LOVE" in its formative first twelve years from its family members, colleagues, friends, home helps, and other acquaintances, but has also been hurt emotionally in its formative first twelve years from its family members, colleagues, friends, home helps, and other acquaintances, and as a result its views of the world are as the Soft individual and is more compliant towards others needs than their own.

It is from my experience and in my humble opinion; that an individual with a SoftSoft PPT is one that exhibits a personality in between the Soft and the SoftSoftSoft, its PPT having being formed by having experienced "ABSOLUTE LOVE" in its formative first twelve years from its family members, colleagues, friends, home helps, and other acquaintances, but having been hurt less emotionally than the SoftSoftSoft individual in its formative first twelve years from its family members, colleagues, friends, home helps, and other acquaintances, such that it views the world as the Soft individual, and its concerns for its own welfare are between those of the Soft and the SoftSoftSoft.

It is from my experience and in my humble opinion; that an individual with a MediumSoft PPT is one that has experienced

"ABSOLUTE LOVE" as the Soft individual, but has also been over indulged, and as a consequence has values similar to that of the Soft individual, but is also manipulative of its family members, colleagues, friends, home helps, and other acquaintances such that it continues to have that feeling of overindulgence throughout its life.

It is from my experience and in my humble opinion; that an individual with a Medium PPT is one that has experienced "ABSOLUTE LOVE" as the Soft individual, but has also been excessively hurt emotionally in its formative first twelve years from its family members, colleagues, friends, home helps, and other acquaintances, and as a result its views of the world are as the Soft individual but also has the need to prove its self worth to negate the feelings of excessive hurt.

It is from my experience and in my humble opinion; that an individual with a MediumHard PPT is one that has not experienced "ABSOLUTE LOVE" as the Soft individual and depending on the degree of "ABSOLUTE LOVE" experienced will view the world as the Soft individual but will also have the need to prop up its self worth with the comparable number of.

It is from my experience and in my humble opinion; that an individual with a MediumHardEgoist PPT is one that has experienced "ABSOLUTE LOVE" in its formative first twelve years from its family members, colleagues, friends, home helps, and other acquaintances, having said it has also been made to feel important such that they are able to show characteristics of all PPTs from the SoftSoftSoft to the MediumHard.

It is from my experience and in my humble opinion; that an individual with a Hard PPT is one that has not experienced "ABSOLUTE LOVE" as the Soft individual, and has only been shown "ABSOLUTE LOVE" by its siblings, such that it's always on the defensive and depending on whom the Hard individual is with, will lash out with narcissistic behavioural patterns as described in Chapter 7 of Book 2, in this Compendium of 3 Books, collectively entitled "Enlightenment - Mother to Daughter"

An individual with a HardHard PPT is one that has had no "ABSOLUTE LOVE", and therefore exhibits no characteristics of the Soft individual, and its recourse in its life is to survive by portraying all narcissistic behavioural patterns as described in Chapter 7 of Book 2, in this Compendium of 3 Books, collectively entitled "Enlightenment - Mother to Daughter".

.

Chapter 2

In this Chapter, Chapter 2 of Book 3 of this Third Book of this Compendium of 3 Books, collectively entitled "Enlightenment - Mother to Daughter", I hope to in my humble opinion; impart how any two individuals can create the most kindest of partnerships such that they are physically, emotionally, mentally, spiritually and socially fulfilled, such that both individuals not only raise offspring that are happy but that both Individuals in this partnership are so content with each other, such that extra marital relationships are not even considered.

In my humble opinion; this can be achieved if both partners in a committed relationship are of a very similar PPT, such that they have common outlooks and understandings, as per in all the previous chapters of this book, having said, it is in my humble opinion; that individuals of dissimilar PPTs can forge ideal partnerships if each other's ideal outlooks are borne in mind and enacted upon.

Chapter 3

In this Chapter, Chapter 3 of this Third Book of this Compendium of 3 Books, collectively entitled "Enlightenment - Mother to Daughter", I would like to in my humble opinion; impart to the reader on the importance of "balance" in any one individual's life.

It is in my humble opinion; that any one individual should work at their revenue generating job four days a week, and spend the other three days of the week on their home life and their interests.

Chapter 4

In this Chapter, Chapter 4 of Book 3 of this Third Book of this Compendium of 3 Books, collectively entitled "Enlightenment - Mother to Daughter", that I would like to impart in my humble opinion; how very important it is that the parents of any newborn child understand that the role of motherhood is second to none. It is in my experience and in my humble opinion; that both parents prior to conceiving understand that the role of motherhood is a necessity till the newborn is aged 12, having said, the role of fatherhood is of consequential importance too.

Chapter 5

In this Chapter, Chapter 5 of this Third Book of this Compendium of 3 Books, collectively entitled "Enlightenment - Mother to Daughter", that I would like to in my experience and in my humble opinion; ask the reader to reflect how partnering with individuals of different cultures and religions can impact on the success of their relationship, as it from my experience and in my humble opinion; that I can say that varying cultures and religions view the sanctimonious roles of motherhood and fatherhood differently.

Lightning Source UK Ltd.
Milton Keynes UK
UKHW011159300321
381250UK00003B/842